Battle For The Bell
The DePauw-Wabash Rivalry

Number 85 Nate Baker got Wabash going early in the 100th Monon Bell Classic. Baker caught only one pass, this 19-yarder in the first quarter, but blocked well in the second half to lead Wabash to victory in the Game of the Century.

David Kogan hurries in to help block downfield. This play set up a 39-yard Alex Costa field goal which got Wabash on the board first in this big game.

DePauw's Jeff Voris scrambling. The Tigers lost a 23-7 lead in the 1986 game, and Voris promised Coach Mourouzis that while he was there DePauw wouldn't lose to Wabash. The Tigers won the next three with Voris at quarterback.

The Wabash College Chapel where thousands of Wabash men have listened to moving speeches and Chapel talks, got married, and got their blood boiling at Monon Bell pep sessions.

East College is one of DePauw's landmark buildings. Students have attended convocations here for over 100 years.

BATTLE FOR THE BELL

The DePauw-Wabash Rivalry

Dick Robinson and Bob New

with

David Haugh

Great Sports Rivalries

Executive Editors: Dick Robinson and Bob New

Publishing assistance by Butler Book Publishing, 3900 Shelbyville Road, Louisville, KY 40207. 502-895-3939.

Printed in Canada

Great Sports Rivalries extends its most sincere appreciation to those who assisted in making *Battle For The Bell* a reality. The efforts of DePauw Sports Information Director Bill Wagner and Wabash Sports Information Director Jim Amidon were especially beneficial. Bill and Jim are the two single most important contributors to the writer, David Haugh, and to Great Sports Rivalries. They represented two fine institutions in a most exemplary manner.

Appreciation is also extended to Mac Thorlton, Director of Alumni Relations for DePauw, and to Gordon Colson, Director of Alumni Affairs for Wabash. Their enthusiasm for the project and their administrative guidance were instrumental to the finished product.

Special credit goes to the photography sources: DePauw University Archives and Special Collections; DePauw University Public Relations; DePauw (Mirage) yearbook; Bill Wagner; and Don Lansu. Also, from Wabash College, photography credit is extended to the Wabash Board of Publications; Wabash News Bureau; Wabash College Yearbooks; and Jim Amidon.

Yea, Bill Butler!

INTRODUCTION

Someone's fist hit the table, shaking several sports writers' coffees.

I heard the pounding and saw the pout only a few rows away. I was baffled.

After all, down below on the Notre Dame Stadium turf, nothing had happened to elicit such a reaction. Charlie Ward hadn't yet missed the open man in the end zone. Bobby Bowden hadn't tried another ill-advised flea-flicker in Notre Dame territory. And Lou Holtz hadn't done much of anything to cause a stir except wear out his usual path of grass on the Notre Dame sidelines.

This was the Game of the Century, Florida State against Notre Dame, No. 1 vs. No. 2, on Nov. 13, 1993. But while NBC was taking a TV timeout, this guy in the press box was taking out his frustration.

"NO!" he shrieked, loud enough to turn heads in his direction. The tiny plug in his ear gave him away. He was listening to another game on another station, I figured, probably a guy from Florida tuning in to find out the Gator score.

This, I was sure, was merely Sunshine State pride in motion.

"Wabash beat DePauw," he announced, in a tone that obviously made him a Tiger fan. The Florida writers looked at each other puzzled. Who?

Wabash beat DePauw. The Monon Bell game.

Huh?

It is a game between two small colleges in central Indiana close to Purdue, in terms of geography and occasionally on the field, too, I joked to an inquiring out-of-stater.

It is the 100th game in the series, I told him. It is popular enough that some cable outlets televised it nationally, I continued. It is the OTHER Game of the Century. It is the OTHER rivalry. It is probably a better game than even this one, I guessed. It is two Division III teams playing like a national championship rested on the outcome. It is players playing with dislocated shoulders, broken bones in their back, bruises, cuts, passion. It is players paying to play, rather than the other way around, and quarterbacks leaving practice early for chemistry labs. It is future doctors, lawyers, bankers and politicians testing their muscle and mettle for the sake of school pride. It is the biggest game of their lives, big enough for a two-time state football champ in the Hoosier state that beating DePauw ranked above those prep accomplishments for him.

It is one of those rare things in society that withstands the test of time; contested as courageously in the roaring '20s, the war-torn '40s and the '60s as it is today. It is a game whose winner won a 350-pound brass bell – The Monon Bell – painted equal parts red and gold for the two participants' school colors.

DePauw's Tony deNicola in the 1985 game.

It is one student body stealing that Bell from the other, using whatever creative method necessary. It is a rivalry of condescending nicknames; Wabash referred to the Tigers as the Dannies, while DePauw countered by labeling the Little Giants as Cavemen or Wallies. It is Wabash defending its all-male enrollment against co-ed DePauw, and vice versa. It is college presidents playing in pep bands, college men leading corny cheers ("Eat Zucchini, Eat, Eat Zucchini!") and quarterbacks hanging in effigy. It is school debates, fraternity parties, yellow leaves and green grass, rustic buildings and dingy weight rooms. It is such big excitement from such a little place. It is so difficult to describe. "It is," I concluded to my Florida friend, "something you just have to be there to appreciate." You understand, I'm sure.

—David Haugh

DePauw cheerleaders had a lot to cheer about in the 1981 game.

Quarterback Jeff Voris calls out the signals in the 1986 game.

The view from the stands: Wabash's #44, Joe Bevelhimer boots an extra point from the hold of Matt Beebe during the 1984 Monon Bell game in Crawfordsville. Wabash won the game 41-26 in front of a frigid, jam-packed crowd of nearly 7,000.

The Wabash team returns from Greencastle with Bell in hand following the 1991 game, which saw Wabash upset the Tigers 23-18.

Wabash unveiled commemorative jerseys for the 100th Monon Bell Classic. A fund-raising effort by Wabash's alumni netted over $60,000 to buy the team personalized jersies. Leading the charge at the start of the 100th game were Chris Wiesehan and Craig Haresty.

CHAPTER ONE

The Significance

Duty called for Pete Metzelaars.

He and his Buffalo Bill teammates gathered at the team's complex on Saturday, November 13, 1993, for another day of films, meetings and strategy sessions. Another mile on the road to another American Football Conference championship needed to be logged. Twelve seasons in the NFL made Metzelaars realize the importance of the upcoming nationally televised Monday night matchup against the Pittsburgh Steelers, a telling late-season test with title implications . . . in hostile territory. Still, on this Saturday, surrounded by videotape players, computer printouts, playbooks and game plans, the only steel Metzelaars could concentrate on was ringing at Blackstock Stadium on the campus of DePauw University in Greencastle, Indiana – about 800 miles and 8 inches of snow from Buffalo.

Nobody involved can quite put into words

what it is about a 350-pound former railroad accessory – the Monon Bell – that turns the mentally fit men from Wabash College and DePauw University into maniacs. But nobody can deny that it does.

Each autumn since 1932, the institution's two football teams clash for the brass clinger in a test of wits and wills that participants swear goes unmatched in college football. The rivalry dates back to 1890, and with each year, and now each century, the stakes seemingly increase.

It is not the Super Bowl, not the Rose Bowl, not even a bowl of any type for these two Division III institutions whose next scholarship athlete will be their first. Yet the game represents college football in its purest form; athletes squeezing the most out of their limited potential in front of friends, relatives and rabid classmates and alumni.

And so often in this series, the expected win-

The 1982 Monon Bell game. A record turned out to see Wabash go undefeated (10-0) with a 31-6 win over DePauw. An estimated crowd of 10,000 turned out on a cold November day.

ners head home despondent while the underdogs dig a little deeper into their wells of resolve and unearth victory.

To the winners go a lifetime of fulfillment and, of course, rights to the treasured Bell. To the losers go, well, disgrace and despair.

Nobody at Wabash, an all-male college of about 800, or DePauw, a co-ed university of about 2,100, remembers much about their senior years, football and non-football students alike, except how their team fared in "The Bell" game. Wabash-DePauw games are recalled by scores more than years.

"Oh, yeah, the 28-8 game, that was a GREAT game," Wabash assistant coach and former wide receiver Scott Boone says, referring to the 1985 Little Giant win. "But that 30-6 game (in 1977), now that was special."

Indeed, they all seem to be to the men of Wabash and

Celebrating Wabash's 1985 win.

18

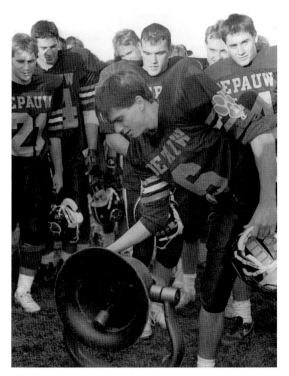

DePauw won the 1989 game 41-14.

DePauw, or DePauw and Wabash, if order matters to you. The intensity of the rivalry is as consistent as autumn's annual coloring of both campuses hues of red, yellow and brown, rustic places that would give Norman Rockwell inspiration.

Maybe it's because the two storied academic institutions sit just 27 miles apart, separated along Hwy. 231 by cornfields, farmhouses and country stores that the games mean so much. The schools represent the main difference between Crawfordsville, Ind., the home of Wabash, in Montgomery County, and Greencastle, in Putnam County. Not much else differs. In both towns, you can buy a custard donut for a quarter. In both towns, a haircut costs less than $10. In both towns, locals brag of the worth of a local education.

In both towns, most of the college men pick from the same co-ed pool. The men of Wabash even have been known to rent a bus for the evenings of Monon Bell games to trans-

Quarterback Rob Doyle leads DePauw past Wabash 21-14 in the 1981 game.

DePauw's equipment manager Frank DeVylder shows the way to the post-game ritual as DePauw wins the 1983 game.

port DePauw women to Crawfordsville for victory parties.

"You wonder why this rivalry is so heated?" asks cagey DePauw athletic director Ted Katula. "Hell, they date the same women."

And, in both towns, no football season can be deemed successful unless the local college team retains temporary ownership of the bell, a weighty chunk of brass mounted on cast iron, that, if it could speak, could spin tales that could keep a convention of narcoleptics up for hours.

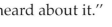

The Monon Bell: Each autumn, Wabash and DePauw alums from Washington D.C. to Washington state hear its echo. That includes lanky tight end alums in Buffalo. "There was a group of guys, Wabash alums, who were getting together the day of the 100th game in Rochester, N.Y., to watch the game on satellite," Metzelaars explains. "It was the 100th. It would have been nice to go watch the game with them, I got an invitation, but I had practice. I got their phone number though.

"So during meetings, we got about two or three breaks. Every break we got, I'd call those guys to keep updated on the score. One of the guys on our team, Billy Brooks, had a brother-in-law playing for DePauw so we both were following the game. He was pulling for DePauw and I was pulling for Wabash. I was glad we (Wabash) won that one or else I would have heard about it."

"I get flak anyway in the locker room for being from Wabash," he adds. "Like after that game, I couldn't get on anybody from Florida State (for losing to Notre Dame on the same day) because they will quickly say, 'How can you say anything when you played at WABASH?' That helps keep me on an even keel."

Metzelaars maintains his allegiance to the Little Giants, especially on those Saturdays they play the terrible Tigers, even if his NFL demands have only allowed him to see one Monon Bell game since his graduation: the '82 game ("31-6") when the NFL players went on strike. After 12 seasons, four Super Bowls, hundreds of receptions and thousands of blocks, losing to DePauw in his senior year of 1981 – his last college game – still stings.

"The thing I remember most about the Bell game is how badly it hurt losing that year because they knocked us out of the playoffs," he says. "That rivalry is as intense as any I've ever seen. The Bills have a big rivalry with the Dolphins. People growing up in Buffalo grow up hating Miami, like Wabash hates DePauw. It used to be, it didn't matter how many games the Bills won, as long as they beat the Dolphins. It's that way with Wabash and DePauw. There's a lot more media coverage and hype in the NFL, but the emotions are just the same at the Bell game. Actually, they may be higher.

"It was big. No question, the rivalry is still a big part of me."

He is not alone. His memories of the series command more attention perhaps because Metzelaars may be the most famous football player to ever battle for the Bell. But as important as the game remains for the Bills' tight end, others possibly put the game on a higher plane not even the 6-foot-7-inch Metzelaars can reach. For them, it is the Super Bowl, because, for them, football ends after their last Monon Bell game.

"Suddenly the boys of autumn had fire in their eyes, Blood and spit, but never quit, fighting for the prize," as The Ballad of the Monon Bell goes. The Ballad was recorded in 1985 by Jim Ibbotson, a member of the Nitty Gritty Dirt Band and a DePauw grad from 1969. DePauw alum Darel Lindquist, class of '68, wrote the Ballad. Before the 100th game, a creative DePauw public relations wordsmith,

The Monon Bell game has significance for the fans as well as the players.

Mike Lillich, revised it in his "Ode to the Monon Bell," "... a friend to man to whom thou say'st, "Victory is truth, truth victory, that is all Ye know on earth, and all ye need to know.'"

Any game that inspires not one, but two ballads must be important. Yet the words "that is all ye know on earth," may not be too far from the truth for the players on both sides; at least for one day, 60 minutes, on a pitch of grass in rural central Indiana. The game consumes all involved, placing everything else on life's back burner, making rational men irrational and honest men liars.

In the 1968 game, for instance, DePauw only led 9-7 at the half. Wabash possessed the better team that season, on meaningless paper, anyway. The Tigers' coach, Tommy Mont, knew it would require something a little extra to hold his lead in the second half. Never a fire-and-brimstone motivator, Mont figured if there ever was a time to rant and

Wabash alumni Dave Parry, '52 (left) and Pete Metzelaars, '82 have an opportunity to visit before a Seattle Seahawks exhibition game at the Indianapolis Hoosier Dome in 1985. Parry is a National Football League referee; Metzelaars played three years with Seattle, catching 27 passes for 304 yards and one touchdown before being traded to the Buffalo Bills before the 1985 season. He remains a star receiver for the Bills.

Nearly the entire student body turned out for the 1993 Monon Bell Pep Session in the Wabash Chapel. In this year the speaker was longtime Wabash professor of speech Joe O'Rourke, who proclaimed, "Dannies dread the Red!"

ABC-TV covered the 1977 Monon Bell game; that's Jim Lampley in the headset.

rave, this was it. After all, this was against Wabash. Enough said.

Mont delivered a speech that shook Knute Rockne's grave, urging his team to maintain the intensity for assistant coach Katula. Because, Mont said with strain in his voice, Katula was leaving the team after the game. The players liked the popular Katula, never at a loss for a story or a smile.

"We were only ahead 9-7 at halftime," recalls DePauw defensive back Mark Dinwiddie, a '70 grad. "Coach Mont, who was never a big motivator, came in at halftime and gave this emotional speech about how this was coach Katula's last year and how we needed to win the game for him. It went on and on."

So did DePauw. Inspired to win one for "Katman," the Tigers roared home from Crawfordsville that day with an 18-7 victory. "And the next year at practice," says Dinwiddie, "there was coach Katula."

If it takes such devious measures, so be it,

former Tiger defensive back Scott Fencik believes. Hey, this is important stuff.

"When it comes to the Wabash game, it's personal," says Fencik, class of '78. "It's as if those guys have done something to your mother, and you're taking it out on anybody in red."

Or, take Boone, as another example. A gentleman in the coaches' office and a smooth-talker on the Wabash recruiting trail, he sees Little Giant red when discussing DePauw. Boone can't help but slip in a few four-letter words to describe his rivals to the south. Occasionally, though, he will use acceptable language. "Put it this way," he says. "When I was being recruited out of high school at Fountain Central (Ind.), DePauw came to look at me. My dad graduated from Wabash. "He told them to never come back."

Then he slipped. "I hate those____!"

Some Wallies, as DePauw likes to call their counterparts, hate Dannies, Wabash's pet nickname for their foes. And vice versa. But most of

The 1983 game ended in a 16-10 DePauw victory as freshman Eric Rawe batted down a Wabash pass as time expired.

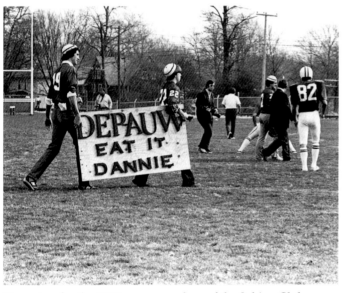

Preparing for the 1982 game, members of the Sphinx Club carry a hand-crafted sign across the field to the home grandstands. 10,000 fans packed into Little Giant Stadium that day to see Wabash beat DePauw 31-6 to cap a perfect 10-0 season.

the hate, according to Katula, comes from the students and the alums. He has seen about 35 Monon Bell games and refuses to believe the reason the intensity level gets as jam-packed as traffic on Hwy. 231 on game day is hate. He prefers to respect his foe, although he will goad the men in red-and-white by saying things like, "Wabash is higher education's answer to (the state penitentiary in) Michigan City."

Katula, dipped in thick black-and-gold

spirit, says he is kidding. More seriously, he knows why he believes the Wabash versus DePauw rivalry holds more meaning than others.

"Our game is special because the type of kid that goes to Wabash and DePauw is very, very similar," he says, rearranging the small model of the Monon Bell on his desk. "They're birds of a feather. Every kid on that field was probably recruited by both teams. No one has a real advantage. It's like looking into a mirror. They may know each other. They may be high school teammates. I know their coaches and their athletic director and they know ours."

Wabash coach Greg Carlson agrees. "You could put two kids, one from each school, into a room and talk to them for hours," Carlson says. "And if they don't tell you and they don't have a uniform on, you won't be able to tell the difference between the two kids. They're so alike."

The familiarity breeds respect more than contempt, at least among players. They don't hate each other. "It's the single-most important athletic event at either place," Katula adds. "Wabash needs to play us, and we need them. It's more important than any national championship at DePauw in any other sport. They are playing for memories that will last an entire lifetime. To think that these two teams may not be playing in 100 years makes me nervous. This is THE game.

"But when the game is over, the game is over. People who handle it best are the players. People think that Wabash hates DePauw and DePauw hates Wabash, but this rivalry exists because of the respect.

"That's what makes the intensity so high."

Just how high is the intensity level? As high as an Ohio State-Michigan matchup? "I want to tell you what," says Katula, who played tight end for Ohio State and coach Woody Hayes in the mid-

26

The Tigers scored 23 second-quarter points to gain a 23-3 halftime lead on the way to a 33-11 win in 1987.

1950s, "there's absolutely no difference between an Ohio State against Michigan game and a Wabash against DePauw game in terms of intensity. Except there may be more in the Bell game."

As high as an Indiana-Purdue game?

"I was involved in some Old Oaken Bucket games," says DePauw coach Nick Mourouzis, an Indiana University assistant in the late '60s, "and the Bell game has a little extra."

As high as Arizona-Arizona State affair?

"Our rivalry against Arizona State is quite strong, almost to the point of not being healthy," explains Dick Tomey, the head coach at Arizona and former DePauw football and baseball player in the late '50s. "But it's such a different scope: There are 90,000 people and a national TV audience watching us. But at DePauw, from our perspective as players then, it was just as intense. And it was. No matter if it's Division I or Division III,

the players want to win. And I've never seen them want to win any more than in that game."

That's high intensity. That's adrenalin helping players do things they've never done before; return a kickoff for a touchdown, block a punt in the end zone, hit receivers on the numbers with pass-rushers in their face, carry the ball until they're so tired it feels heavy.

That's Wabash versus DePauw.

That's life in the Monon Bell series. "I remember one year we were 8-1, flying high as can be," Katula says, scratching his head. "And we lost to a Wabash team we should have beaten to make us 8-2. The football banquet that year was like a wake.

"Then, maybe the very next year, we were 4-5-1, a lousy year. But we beat Wabash. It was amazing how much better the food tasted at that banquet."

27

CHAPTER TWO

The History

Squatting behind his center, Stuart Smith shouted. "Nine-seventy-six . . .Eighty-four . . Thirty-two . . . Fifty-one . . .Hike."

The eight called for a shift right.

The four called for the trailing halfback to get the handoff.

The sequence of numbers called for the back to hit the hole between the left guard and tackle, however wide or narrow it may be.

Nothing in the Wabash quarterback's cadence called for his tailback to slip four yards behind the line of scrimmage. That, Smith and his Little Giant teammates could not afford. This was fourth down on the 1-yard line with three minutes remaining in the fourth quarter of a critical game that was tied, 0-0. And this was no ordinary critical game, this was against DePauw, on the Tigers' frigid home turf, in front of 2,500 loyal, freezing

fans who crowded as close to the charcoal burners on the sidelines as possible. This, for the first time, was for the Monon Bell. This was November 1932.

Interest in the Wabash vs. DePauw game rose higher than the usual wave that autumn, because, for the first time, the winner of the game earned rights to a 350-pound bell donated by the Monon Railroad. It seems a DePauw alum from the '20s, Orien W. Fifer had penned a plea to Indianapolis News sports editor William F. Fox suggesting that a trophy be awarded to the Wabash-DePauw winner similar to the Little Brown Jug or the Old Oaken Bucket. Because the railroad connected Crawfordsville and Greencastle like links on a chain, a natural symbol of the series was born.

According to DePauw legend, university publicity director Russell Alexander presented the bell at a chapel pep session the day before the game

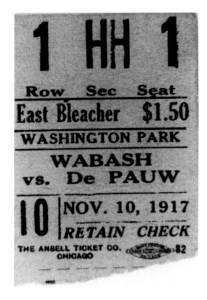

as the official trophy for the game. DePauw gained initial ownership of the bell, painted half "Old Gold," and half "Wabash Scarlet," by virtue of the Tigers' 13-7 victory in 1931.

But 1932 brought a new game, with new hope, with new heroes, with a new symbol to play for. . .and a foot of new snow on Blackstock Field.

The playing surface was a mess. DePauw coach Gaumey Neal and the Tiger athletic department asked the male students for help in clearing the field from the late-autumn dusting of snow. For two days leading up to the game, the men used

Edmund F. Ball, Wabash Class of 1927, joins former football players from both schools during halftime ceremonies of the 100th game. Ball played on some of Pete Vaughn's all-time best squads. Below, Wabash vs. Depauw in the 1920s.

Leather helmets and a lack of padding did not diminish the intensity of the rivalry in the '20s.

scoop shovels, horses and hay wagons in sub-freezing temperatures to get rid of about 10 inches of snow. The wagon wheels and horses dug grooves in the field that made the footing horrendous. Even DePauw's legendary halfback Don Wheaton, compared by sports writers to Red Grange, found the going sloppy; Wabash's defense limited him to negative yardage.

With Wheaton went DePauw's chances. The Tigers' only hopes rested with their defense, a cold and tired unit that found itself giving up ground to the Wabash offensive line late in the fourth quarter.

Now the ball sat inside the 1-yard line, a mere 12 inches from a sure Wabash victory, which would be the Little Giants' first in the series since 1929. Twelve inches.

Smith called his cadence and took the snap with his frozen fingers. The weary DePauw defensive line wilted. The hole opened. It was wide

enough to wedge the 350-pound bell through. Little Giant running back Red Varner could have walked through the opening as casually as if he were walking to English class back on the Crawfordsville campus.

But he slipped. Then he fell. DePauw ball. And nobody won the game – or the bell. After the 0-0 tie, fitting isn't it, the bell went to DePauw, only because the Tigers had won the previous meeting in 1931. It stayed in Greencastle in 1933 when DePauw's unbeaten, unscored-upon team, the only one in college football since, posted a 14-0 victory over Wabash in Crawfordsville. For the first time, the Monon Bell rightfully belonged in the winners' camp.

Before the winning team earned rights to the bell, the only prize at stake in the game was pride. As if that wasn't enough.

Both institutions began football in 1884, but didn't meet each other on the field until 1890. From

31

A DePauw Tradition

The 1933 Football Team
Undefeated, untied and unscored upon ...

the opening kickoff that November 22 afternoon, it became clear that this was no game for the meek of heart. DePauw based its decision whether to keep the program for another year on the outcome of the Wabash game. Wrote the school newspaper after the Tigers' 34-5 win in 1890: "Had DePauw lost to Wabash, it would have been with the greatest difficulty that a sentiment favorable to football and the right to support a team next year could have been worked up next season."

But sentiment grew. And so did the personal, biting nature of the series. In 1895, the "DePauw Weekly," accused Wabash of buying off the referees. "The best of teams can't win when playing against 13 men," it wrote. The story goes that a DePauw player recovered a fumble only to have the official, supposedly a friend of the Wabash coach, award the ball to the Little Giants.

Wabash also gets credit – or perhaps blame – for starting the pranks that so characterize the series. In 1900, a man claiming to be a reporter from the Indianapolis Press obtained permission from

Good pass coverage along the sideline in this game in the '30s.

the DePauw manager to cover a game from the Tiger bench in order to be more comprehensive. When DePauw arrived in Crawfordsville a week later for its next game against Wabash, the Tigers discovered that the reporter was actually Mr. Anthony Chez . . . the coach of Wabash.

Despite criticizing Chez for his deception, the DePauw folks didn't learn. Or didn't care. The next year, the Tigers hired Chez as their head football coach.

A few years later, in 1904, relations between

An aerial view of the Wabash campus in 1930.

the two schools soured even more. Wabash walloped every team in its path early that season; Hanover 81-0, Earlham 35-0, Butler 51-0. And one of the Little Giants' players, Bill Cantrell, was black. In those days, in central Indiana, it may have been more acceptable to see a woman in shoulder pads and a helmet than a black man. DePauw president Bishop Edwin Hughes objected and canceled the Thanksgiving Day game between the teams.

The same possibility of cancellation existed a year earlier because of the presence of Wabash player Sam S. Gordon, also black. But General Lew Wallace, a Civil War general and the author of "Ben Hur" who graduated from Wabash in 1840, stuck his unbiased nose into the situation and ordered that the game be played. So it was.

But when nobody intervened in 1904, DePauw chose instead to play Wabash Athletic Association from Wabash, Ind. The Tigers, predict-

ably, won 6-0 and for years claimed a win over Wabash that season until research clarified the matter. The next season, 1905, Wabash took out two years of frustration with a 52-0 flattening of the Tigers, the second of eight straight games in the series without a loss.

The only other time after that the teams didn't meet in a season came in 1910, when the game wasn't played because of the tragic death of Wabash player Ralph Wilson. A St. Louis University player struck Wilson's head with his knee, fracturing his skull in three places. He died the next morning and his family buried him under a tombstone at Oak Hill Cemetery that expressed his last words and read, "Ralph Lee Wilson 1891-1910... Did Wabash Win?"

Wabash did win during most of the '20s, posting an 8-2 mark during the decade. In the '30s, when the Bell rivalry began, DePauw came back to win six times, Wabash twice and the teams also tied twice.

DPU and Wabash pile up within inches of the goal line during the 1932 traditional battle.

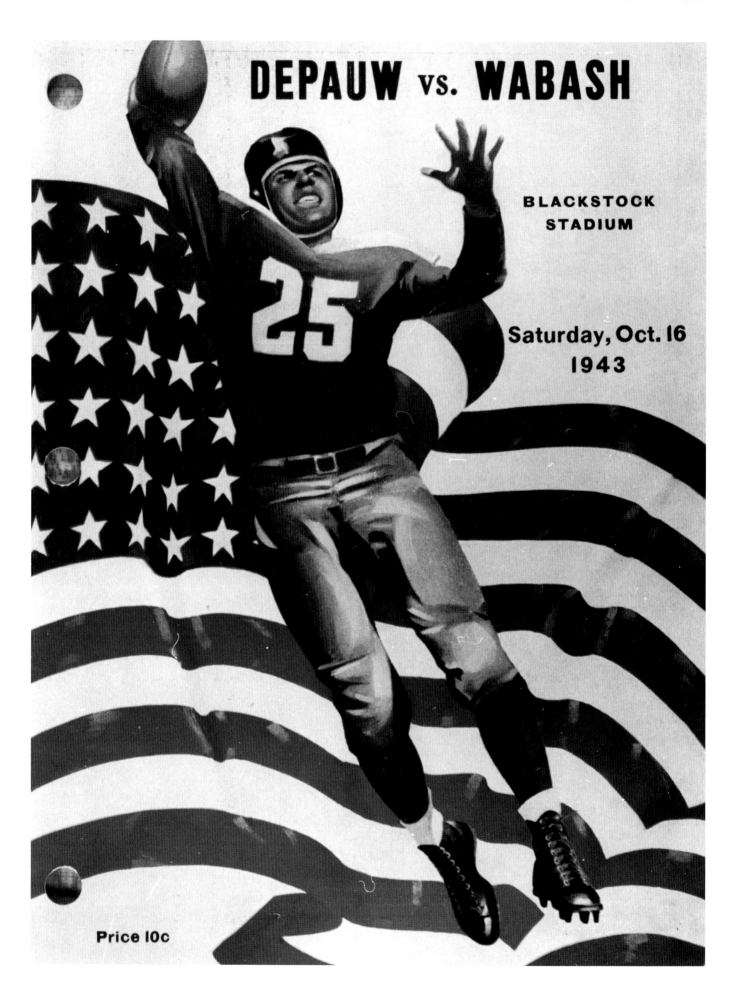

DEPAUW vs. WABASH

BLACKSTOCK STADIUM

Saturday, Oct. 16
1943

Price 10c

34

Coach Pete Vaughn holds class with some of the team just prior to a game in the 1940s.

World War II did little to dampen the spirit of the rivalry in the '40s; in fact, it enhanced it. With the two institutions serving as training sites for the Navy, some of the fittest men in the country fought for the Monon Bell. Some of the funniest, too. Norman Knights, a DePauw grad from 1944, quipped at a roast before the 1943 game: "Half of the DePauw class marries each other. With Wabash, it's only 10 percent."

Wabash enjoyed the last laugh that decade; winning six and losing four. In fact, the Little Giants had won six straight before a faked injury

Gaumey Neal coached the Tigers for 16 seasons, including the undefeated campaigns of 1933 and 1943. The 1933 team was the last in college football to go undefeated, untied, and unscored-on.

bailed DePauw out in 1955.

Fraternity brothers will do anything for each other. And DePauw kicker Fred Williams, not to mention the rest of his Tiger teammates, needed a favor. A big favor. The score between Wabash and DePauw was tied at 20 with time ticking away. DePauw had no timeouts left. Suddenly, DePauw's Gene Halladay, a Sigma Chi fraternity brother of Williams, lay in pain. He was injured, or so the officials thought. The clock stopped. The ball sat on the 19-yard line. Time existed for one more play, a field goal, DePauw's first attempt of the season.

The Tigers called on "Fearless Fred" Williams. He connected on the 19-yarder into the south end zone. Bedlam reigned. Fans and students tore down the goal posts. Players and coaches hugged. And, remarkably, Halladay's injury vanished.

"But the thing that really made the kick and the victory so memorable," recalls Williams, re-nicknamed "Golden Toe" after the kick, "was that (DePauw) President Humbert gave the whole student body an extra day off at Thanksgiving."

Tiger cheerleader Rae Lahti Donnelly still is grateful to Williams. "As I recall," she says, "we had that extra day off all four years I was at DePauw. When I think of the bell, I have to admit the first thing I think of is the extra day off."

The '55 victory brought the Bell back to Greencastle, where it stayed for 10 years. Since Wabash's 16-6 victory ended the DePauw streak in '65, the legend of the bell has become richer as media and sports have assumed a greater role in society. The game has been featured twice on the pages of Sports Illustrated, has been televised by regional cable outlets and ESPN2 contacted the schools about broadcasting the 101st game of the series. Even Charles Kuralt chronicled the personality of the series on his "Sunday Morning" show.

The competitive balance has lived up to the increased hype; the series was tied at 33-33-7 in

1966 and again was tied at 45-45-9 before the 100th meeting in 1993.

In between, heroes were made and dreams were fulfilled. There was the Mud Bowl of '67; the Tigers' goal-line stand in '70; the hard-nosed running of DePauw's Bart Simpson, the running back, not the cartoon runt; the Stan Parrish Era at Wabash when the Little Giants made national headlines; the storied career of future NFL star Pete Metzelaars; more nail-biting tie games; the seemingly annual '80s battles for Division III playoff positions; the field goal by Wabash's Alex Costa in '92 that evened the series after 99 meetings . . .

"You gotta taste it once," says DePauw quarterback Jeff Voris, class of '90.

Once wouldn't have been enough for Greencastle restaurateur Marvin Long, if that once came in 1986. A diehard DePauw fan, Long watched in horror as the Tigers squandered a 23-6 lead with 4 minutes left in the fourth quarter. In the game, DePauw outgained Wabash 452-186. With just over a minute left, the Little Giants took a 24-23 lead but DePauw stormed back. The Tigers final drive stalled at the Wabash 19-yard line because DePauw couldn't stop the clock to get the

The DePauw Tigers prepare for action in the 1940s.

field-goal unit on the field to kick a certain game-winner. "

"(DePauw coach) Nick (Mourouzis) didn't have any timeouts left and couldn't get the field goal off," Long says. "That's when we started calling Coach Mourouzis "Timeout Nick." It was a great ballgame, exciting as hell."

Most of the Monon Bell games in the 20th century have been. And lately, most have also been just as profitable for the athletic departments.

In 1982, for instance, over 9,500 fans flooded Little Giant Stadium to see Wabash maintain its undefeated record with a 31-6 defeat of DePauw. The game generated a record $18,341 in gate receipts.

Investing in a $5 ticket usually pays off.

"It's the most unpredictable game you could possibly imagine," retired DePauw professor Charlie Erdmann explains in the university's alumni magazine. "It doesn't matter whether the teams have winning or losing records, they both get up for this game like no other."

Bob Steuber led the nation in scoring while at Missouri and even played for the Chicago Bears prior to spending the 1943 season at DePauw as part of the Navy's V-5 program.

Morrie Goodnight finds the end zone in the 1955 game which was won on a last-second field goal by Fred "The Toe" Williams.

The motto for the DePauw Tigers says it all.

In 1959 it was "like kissing your sister", in the mud yet, as the Monon Bell game ended in a tie. Here Scotty Polizotto tries to gain yardage for Wabash.

Wabash's George "Rainbow" Trout scores the Little Giant's only touchdown in a 37-6 DePauw win in 1957.

The offensive line of Coach Walt Bartkiewicz made a name for itself in the 28-0 Cavemen win in 1954.

They simply heed the age-old advice of Francis Mitchell Cayou, the Wabash coach from 1904 until 1908. The Omaha Indian actually provided Wabash the nickname "Little Giants," because of the way his team performed against larger schools like Notre Dame. To wit: The Indians, Wabash's former nickname, beat the Irish in 1905. Cayou's words of wisdom: "Will you be a man or a trembling fawn? Grip the ball carrier as the great bear grips. Break him. Close in on the carrier as does the wolf pack!"

Intense enough? And that was in 1904. Yet, like wine, the Monon Bell series has become even finer and more pure with age.

*Brothers Dave Joyce, DePauw quarterback, and Doug Joyce, end,
pose with the Monon Bell prior to a '50s clash.*

(Above) Coach Tom Mont guided the Tigers to a 12-5-1 record in Monon Bell matchups.

(Left) Fred "The Toe" Williams secured his place in Monon Bell history by kicking the game-winning field goal in the 1955 classic.

The DePauw faithful watch Monon Bell action in the 1950s.

The referee keeps a sharp eye on the action in the 1956 Monon Bell battle.

41

Stan Huntsman ran for two TD's and passed for another in the 1952 Little Giant 47-0 romp over DePauw. Huntsman gained over 2,700 yards in his stellar career at Wabash.

ATTENTION KITTY KATS

"Too bad," said the Caveman to
The Tiger from old D.P.U.,
"Your many losses will be increased
When Wabash leaves your cat deceased."

Advice to Tigers, "Make your will
Before you leave for Crawfordsville."
And this old adage, please note too,
"To hell with you old D.P.U.!!!"

Nov. 1951

From November, 1951.

(Right) The 1952 Little Giants.

(Below) Fans like these helped keep the Bell away from Wabash for a decade, from 1955 to 1964.

43

It's "Dad's Day" at DePauw for the 1965 game.

John Butler, DePauw sophomore in 1965, eludes a Wabash tackler.

Head Coach Max Urick's Little Giants entered the 1967 Monon Bell game in Greencastle with a 1-7 record, while DePauw was 6-1-1 and heavily favored. But Wabash won, 7-0 in the Mud Bowl, and the Monon Bell, which had been buried in the frozen, muddy end zone, returned to Crawfordsville.

(Above) Ball carrier Wayne Monroe looks for some blocking ahead in the 1967 Bell game. Monroe was the star of the game, gaining 143 yards in Wabash's 7-0 victory.

(Left) A 350-pound bell makes a fine climbing structure for kids on the DePauw campus.

(Below) Little Giant John May (45) sweeps left in the 1965 Monon Bell 16-6 Wabash victory.

DePauw 17, Wabash 7 in the snow in 1969.

(Below) The end of the famous Mud Bowl, 1967.

(Above) Members of the Wabash College pep band, decked out in sweaters with their class years on the front, entertain students at the annual Monon Bell Pep Session prior to the 1967 Monon Bell game. Bob Mitchum directs the band.

(Left) The DePauw defense and the mud made it tough for Wabash ball carriers in the 1962 Monon Bell game. DePauw won 13-10.

CHAPTER THREE

The Heists

Even the most religious gym rats sleep.

So Don Money knew that the bodies he saw walking onto the steps of Chadwick Court on the Wabash College campus at 2:30 a.m. Sunday, September 19, 1993, weren't trying to cure their insomnia by shooting baskets. He sensed mischief. And, after 19 years of patroling those parts as a Wabash security guard, Money's instincts usually were, um, on the money.

He stood nearby, about a football field away, when three shadows entered the building that stores the Monon Bell. Money followed. He spied a young man climbing onto the mantle where the bell was attached. The perpetrator returned the look. "Someone's coming," yelled Matt Ingle, the DePauw student who had climbed the gym walls with the intent of stealing the Monon Bell.

Stealing the Bell has become another sporting event between the DePauw and Wabash. Monon Bell Heist, the participants call it. The rules are simple: the theft must occur in the fall, because confiscating the Bell in a season other than football season would be like celebrating Christmas in May; no thrills, no anticipation. The other rule, for safety purposes, prohibits the use of weapons other than the imagination, which, with this group, can be quite a tool. A final rule states that the Bell must be returned before kickoff that autumn. The bell has unceremoniously changed hands and homes more times than anyone can count. The first official report of a stolen Monon Bell dates back to 1941, when the practice of awarding the Bell to the winner of the game was just 9 years old.

Wabash authorities, in possession of the Bell at the time, reported the 350-pound object missing. A three-week investigation uncovered nothing but frustration. With nobody suspecting the Tigers, Wabash officials figured that thieves stole the Bell to sell because of its scrap iron value. Of course, they figured wrong.

Nobody in stuffed shirts and silk ties gets too bothered about the regular attempts by students to steal the Bell. Most view the practice as another rite of passage for college men at Wabash and DePauw; orientation, final exams, fraternity parties, graduation and the Monon Bell Heist. In fact, longtime Wabash athletic director Max Servies nearly beams when he discusses his students' ability to not only seize the Bell, but protect it, too. "We don't have to worry about security," Servies says with a sly grin. He obviously wasn't around in 1941. "But the guys at DePauw," he adds, "they have a different problem."

At least Ingle and his two DePauw accomplices caught in the darkness of Chadwick Court with Money wouldn't argue. Problems? They had plenty. Here they were, at 2:30 in the morning in arch-enemy territory, pulling off a heist for Tiger pride. And a 63-year-old security guard decided to take a stroll across campus the exact time they entered the home address of the Monon Bell. They cursed their luck, among other things.

Knowing no 63-year-old could keep pace with three college-aged men, the conspirators fled the scene of the attempted theft. Ingle jumped about eight feet to the floor and darted out the south lobby doors with his friends. Two more accomplices waited for them in a 1984 Subaru station wagon.

Money had seen the vehicle earlier parked on the street. So he headed for it through a back

Wabash fans, shouting "Beat the Dannies" and "Eat zuchinni" parade in front of the visitors' stands at Greencastle's Blackstock Stadium. The Sphinx Club, a Wabash service and spirit club, is usually in charge of transporting the Monon Bell to and from games when it is in the possession of the Little Giants.

Members of the Sphinx Club carry the Bell from the DePauw sideline after Wabash's upset victory, 28-8, in 1985.

way, realizing he couldn't win a footrace with the fugitives. "After all," Money says. "What would I do if I caught them anyway?"

The DePauw students piled into the car as Money neared from the other direction. The driver couldn't start the car. Each failed try gave Money another step. When it finally started, the car slowly got away. But too slowly. Money shined his flashlight onto the license plate and wrote down the numbers.

He returned to the gym to survey the damage, but there had been none. Then he called the police and reported the license plate numbers. Police traced the car to Ingle's dad, Stephen, and Matt turned himself in the next day. Arrested and fingerprinted, the DePauw sophomore spent 45 minutes in the Montgomery County Jail. He paid $400 in bond and $110 for a first-offender program that

reduced his charge from a felony to a misdemeanor. His friends avoided prosecution. Ingle also wasn't allowed to show his face in Crawfordsville for six weeks, not that he would want to do so.

"I expected a slap on the wrist or a lecture," Ingle told *Sports Illustrated*. "We didn't see it as stealing. We were just trying to return the bell to its rightful owners."

In Money's mind, it was already there. And the responsibility of keeping it there belonged to him, a shield of honor for Wabash security staffers if completed successfully.

"Oh, no, it's never been stolen when I was working," Money says proudly. "That would be kind of an embarrassment if the bell was stolen while you're on duty."

Though Money escaped Bell Heist embar-

A few ingenious Wabash students borrowed the DePauw University sign for display purposes on the Wabash College campus before the 1980 clash.

rassment, former DePauw president Dr. William H. Kerstetter didn't. His gaffe in 1965 made legend and the incident remains the standard by which all other Monon Bell heists are measured.

The fine print read "Noblesville Daily Ledger." But DePauw athletic director James Loveless didn't read the fine print. Nor did President Kersetetter or either of the two pretty Tiger co-eds who were summoned to take a picture around the Monon Bell with a Mexico City News reporter. Everybody assumed that when the reporter flashed his press card, the small letters spelled "Mexico City News," and not "Noblesville Daily Ledger." How wrong they were.

For Jim Shanks, a Wabash College sophomore, was not a Mexican reporter, as he claimed, or any reporter at all. He was a Little Giant football fan carrying out an elaborate, ingenious plan to steal the Monon Bell. Shanks had arranged a lunch with Kerstetter under the premise that he was a foreign reporter researching colleges for a brochure. Kerstetter welcomed Shanks, discussing everything from American culture to the color of the DePauw owl with him over lunch. When the president left the table, he had, at Shanks' behest, agreed to supply at least one scholarship to needy Latin-American students desperate to attend college in America, students, in reality, who didn't exist.

Shanks and Kerstetter met later in the afternoon when the student reporter asked if he could take a picture home to Mexico of the famous Monon Bell. "My gosh," Kerstetter said, "Why didn't I think of that?"

Kerstetter didn't know where the Bell was hidden so he asked his secretary. "The last time I told a visitor where the Bell was," she said, "it was stolen." Little did she know . . .

A more skeptical Loveless actually agreed to show Kerstetter and his media companion to

Wabash students guard the coveted Bell prior to the 1953 clash.

the bell, even offering to supply two female DePauw students to spruce up the photo. Loveless, slightly nervous, asked for credentials from Shanks. He quickly flashed a card that nobody bothered to look at closely; like the con man who flashes a fake badge in the movies.

The group walked over to the second floor of the maintenance building near Blackstock Stadium, where the Bell was hidden under some barrels. Several photos were snapped and Shanks thanked the president and his friends before heading home. His hosts thought home meant Mexico when, in fact, it meant Crawfordsville.

That night, with precious knowledge of the whereabouts of the Bell, Shanks and three friends drove the same car he used in the afternoon onto the Greencastle campus. Authorities noticed and

The Bell in DePauw's protective custody in the 1970s.

told the group to leave town. With police diverted by Shanks, another group of Wabash men broke into the maintenance building and seized the Bell.

Kerstetter knew he had been had and the Bell had been taken back to Crawfordsville, but "I don't know where."

A few hours before the game that year, Wabash Dean of Students Norman Moore returned the Bell to DePauw, following an unofficial Heist rule. Wabash regained legitimate possession of the Bell later that afternoon with a 16-6 victory. Excited Little Giant fans, aware of the circumstances of the Heist, wore Mexican ponchos and sombreros when they walked onto the field in the postgame celebration. And Jim Shanks walked into Wabash legend as the unparalleled king of Monon Bell thefts.

There have been other thieves and other thefts, though maybe none as shrewd or cunning as Shanks.

But certainly, whoever buried the Bell in the north end zone of Blackstock Stadium in 1967 pondered long and hard over that decision. Apparently, a group of DePauw students stole the Bell from their alma mater after the Tigers' '66 win to keep it from characters like Shanks. For 11 months, folks thought the Bell was missing. Then during the third quarter of the '67 Mud Bowl, workers dug it out of a pile of lumber at the north end zone of the stadium. The home fans only were able to pull the Bell around the Stadium once before the loathed Little Giants resumed temporary ownership with a 7-0 victory.

At times, stealing the Bell can get downright dangerous. Former DePauw strong safety Randy Wells recalls an

Monon Bell memories. Little Giant fans gather around to see the Monon Bell, which had been stolen from DePauw before the 1965 game in the scam known as "the Mexican Heist."

The Monon Bell under heavy guard in Greencastle.

evening outside the Sigma Nu fraternity house in Greencastle in 1978 when things got out of hand. Because about 60 percent of the Tiger football team, at that time, belonged to the Sigma Nu fraternity, DePauw stored the Bell at the house. What better place to protect the Bell than keep it where the people who won it lived? The Wabash players learned where the Bell was. To seize it, they chose force over finesse.

A "bunch of carloads" of Little Giants – actually about 300 students – trekked south to Greencastle to storm the Sigma Nu house. In all, 11 students were arrested in the scuffle.

"A wrestler came through the door," Wells says, "and somebody broke his leg."

Ouch. Imagine if that someone was a football player as important as Pete Metzelaars. It could have been. More incidents like that one occurred later that decade and beyond. Once, Metzelaars found himself right in the middle of the action, and he felt as comfortable as if he were running a drag route between two linebackers.

Metzelaars, who played from '78-'81, was one of about 500 Little Giants who lumbered into

Greencastle with the sole intent of regaining their stolen Bell. He says Wabash retrieved it; others challenge his story. Who's to argue with someone 6-foot-7 and 255 pounds? "All I remember," Metzelaars says, "is that it was a lot of fun to do that."

DePauw officials and students arrange a safe transfer back to campus after the Bell was stolen yet again.

Neither Metzelaars nor anyone else in Little Giant red-and-white had much fun trying to get the Bell back in August of 1979. So, of course, Wabash turned to trickery. But only after DePauw had coaxed them into it. A group of DePauw students got some laughs when they sneakily seized the Bell and hid it in Greencastle before football season started. For bargaining power, a few industrious Wabash men sneaked into selected DePauw fraternity parties and helped themselves to merchandise laying around the grounds. An exchange of the stolen items eventually was arranged between the conspirators.

Fun also motivated a group of unidentified Wabash men to hide in DePauw's Lilly Center until security personnel left the building in 1988 after a Tiger home basketball victory over the Little Giants. The men took cover in the area of the building where the Tiger track team stored their Port-A-Pit mats. Another Wabash group in a silver Mercedes station wagon would meet them at the

rear door of the basketball court at 1:30 a.m. They would bring with them from Crawfordsville a blow torch, three crowbars, a sledge hammer, duct tape, towels, five two-by-fours, a power saw, an extension cord and a tool box. When the coast became clear, the students unbolted the Bell, lowered it from its 12-foot-high perch, and dropped it onto one of the Port-A-Pit mats.

It took a two of the Wabash men to load the Bell on a cart, where it was pushed across the court, out the door and into the Mercedes.

Someone once said that the feeling of exhilaration thieves get after successfully stealing the Monon Bell matches the feeling players get after winning the game. It was that feeling that group of students reveled in on the short drive back to Crawfordsville after their Bell Heist. Others, like Shanks, have felt it, too.

It was that feeling that escaped Matt Ingle in September 1993. For the time being. "I hear the guy they put in jail that time said he would try to steal it again from Wabash," says Money, Ingle's senior-citizen nemesis. "He's welcome to try."

Consider that an open invitation, if not a challenge. And if Ingle declines, bet that someone, sometime will RSVP in his place. Soon.

After the 1984 Monon Bell game.

CHAPTER FOUR

The Support

Jim Kilbane had made the same read, stepped into the same hole, delivered the same teeth-chattering blow in the same scarlet Wabash jersey with the same ferocity hundreds of times before. Thousands of times. But all those other times, shoulder pads protected the linebacker. So did a helmet, a face mask, knee pads and elbow pads.

This time, though, Kilbane had nothing but a mouthpiece and his good judgment to help protect him from injury. And intensity – good ol' fashioned "Killer" Kilbane intensity – nudged good judgment aside.

"Marv Flewellen, a DePauw running back from the '80s ('82-'84) was running through the hole when I met him and tried to form tackle like I

always did," Kilbane says. "I've done that a bunch of times and instinct took over. So I did, and brought my head first. But I forgot something, I forgot to stop. My nose hit on his head and there was blood everywhere."

Kilbane broke his nose. That nose, with the rest of his head, was exposed because flag-football players don't wear helmets. And that's what Kilbane was when he tackled Flewellen in the annual Monon Bell Alumni Football game, a function recently woven neatly into the tradition of the rivalry between Wabash and DePauw.

The alumni flag-football game started in 1982 by DePauw graduate Don Popravak, the president of the DePauw Alumni Football Club. Popravak, an '81 graduate, possesses a passion for

Record crowd turns out to see Wabash go undefeated (10-0) with a 31-6 win over DePauw in the 1982 Bell game.

the DePauw football program, which means he can't escape memories of the Monon Bell series. His last game as a Tiger, the 22-22 tie in 1980 in Crawfordsville sent Popravak off to graduation unfulfilled. "None of us had ever been in a tie before," he recalls. "We wandered around out on the field after the game not really knowing what to do."

His thirst for Wabash competition remained unquenched. So, one day in 1982, a group of DePauw grads squared off against a group of Wabash grads in a touch-football game in the Lincoln Park area of Chicago. They called it the Little Monon Bell game, an affair meant to gather alums from both schools living in the Chicagoland area.

"I had unfinished business to do," Popravak says. "I wanted to play again. I just didn't see why football had to end with our collegiate careers."

Now, thanks to Popravak, Kilbane and about 100 other willing alums from both sides, their careers continue once each year in a fun and physical game of flag-football. Winners receive a miniature Monon Bell.

Though the site of the game originally was Chicago, so the large number of Wabash and DePauw alums in the area could participate, the battle has since moved to the campus site of the actual Monon Bell game each fall. The reasoning: Holding the alumni game near the stadium of the college game may spark more interest in the old-timers' game while making another show of support to the current programs.

Sometimes, one game resembles the other.

Kilbane, Wabash's all-time leading tackler with 400 in four seasons, never injured himself badly in college. He approached the game the way many middle linebackers did – in a bad mood. If he suffered a bump or a bruise, he usually played through the pain.

But in about a decade of roaming sideline-to-sideline as a flag-football linebacker, Kilbane has broken his nose and his finger and also received a concussion from bumping heads with an opposing running back, probably Flewellen again. Obviously, the linebacker who never lost a home game in four years at Wabash takes his flag-football as seriously.

"The game maintains a wonderful intensity," Kilbane says. "It's a chance to settle old scores you never had a chance to settle. But it really goes beyond settling a score. Even when you grow up and mature in life, the (Monon Bell) rivalry stays with you. It never dies. For it to be rekindled for 90 minutes on a brisk, cold Saturday morning once a year is worth it. It's definitely worth it to rekindle those old memories. For me, it's cathartic.

"You may be a step slower and a pound heavier, but you still have that . . . wantonness for the opponent. So you don't allow yourself to let up. Because you really feel, deep down, that they represent a different genre than what you represent.

"It goes way beyond Bruce Springsteen and the song, 'Glory Days.' You wouldn't do this against just anybody. But you would against DePauw."

The feeling, rest assured, is mutual on the DePauw side. "No one wants to lose the alumni

Long a part of Monon Bell madness, the Wabash Pep Band always makes the trip to Greencastle for the Monon Bell game. In this photo from 1985, former Wabash president Dr. Lewis Salter (in tie) takes a break from playing drums, which he also did during his tenure as president.

game," explains former Tiger quarterback Tony deNicola. "In the first half, it's more friendly, kind of joking around and stuff. But in the second half, if the outcome of the game is still hanging in the balance, then it can get pretty ugly."

When it gets ugly in the second half, the alums closest to their former playing weight take over. Before crunch time, anyone with a degree from either institution may get a chance to play. You don't have to be a former football player to break a sweat in the Alumni Game; it's designed to build camaraderie as much as provide competition.

DePauw and Wabash grads from the '50s routinely show up to take a few snaps. Old stars like Kilbane, deNicola, David Broecker, Alan Hill and others regularly show up to relive history. Even graduates from both institutions who never earned a varsity letter put on a jersey for the alumni game, curious to smell the enthusiasm of the Bell rivalry. "It really gets a lot of

Nick Mourouzis came to DePauw in 1981 and won his first Bell game, 21-14.

Wally Wabash leads the fans onto the field before the Bell game in the early '70s.

older players interacting with younger guys," Popravak says. "It helps the younger guys make contacts and maybe even get a job down the road.

"The original goal of the game was to continue the spirit of the Monon Bell rivalry. In many different ways, I think it has."

The spirit of the Bell lives through other bodies of the university family, too. The connection people on each campus feel to their football programs differs from most campus settings. Because players and coaches usually are close enough to touch and talk to, and not locked away in some football-only dormitory or laboring for four hours a day on the back practice field, people on each campus assume an ownership of their team people on bigger campuses can't possibly assume.

The support shows.

Sure, other programs sponsor pep clubs, cheerleading groups and other support groups, but the folks at DePauw and Wabash swear the students and alums who crank up the hype machine before the Monon Bell game each year stand alone.

Even a college football coach involved in a 1993 game dubbed "The Game of the Century," took time out of his busy week to write the DePauw team a letter of encouragement before the 100th Wabash-DePauw game, as per Popravak's request. Notre Dame coach Lou Holtz, only a few days before his Irish catapulted to the No. 1 spot in college football with a 31-24 victory over Florida State, when every minute and hour mattered to Holtz, sent his best wishes to the Tigers. Wrote Holtz: "You are playing the greatest game in the world. It is not a Constitutional right to play football, but a privilege . . .and with this privilege goes the responsibility of maintaining a commitment to excellence . . . "If you think like a winner, act like a winner, and behave like a winner, YOU WILL BE A WINNER. Good luck."

Wally Wabash greets a regional TV audience in 1977.

Some people think the real Monon Bell game is this one—the now-annual flag football game between the schools' alumni.

This DePauw flag football team looks like it could still play varsity ball.

Even from coaches uninvolved, the Monon Bell Rivalry brings out such enthusiasm. It's Wally Wabash, the Little Giants' mascot, versus the cute corps of Tiger cheerleaders, a luxury all-male Wabash can't match. It's the Cavemen of Wabash versus the Dannies of DePauw in the annual debate between the two schools, featuring arguments persuasive enough to lure cats to a kennel. It's Homecoming, the Sphinx Club, the pep band, spirit rallies, bon fires, Monon Bell concerts, fraternity parties . . .

It's the Wabash masculinity versus the DePauw intellect, or the other way around, depending on whom you ask. Either way, the people on both campuses drink up the euphoria. "I couldn't believe how much the student bodies got into the game," former DePauw coach Tom Mont recalls. "Coaching at the University of Maryland, we had student involvement, but it's a detached involvement. At DePauw, it's different. I knew almost every student I saw. I would pass the same ones on the courtyard every day. You get to know them and they get to know you."

Almost too well. Sometimes the fans get so caught up in the excitement of the game that they overstep their bounds. Wabash coach Greg Carlson can vouch for that. Carlson likes football to be all business, especially during the week of the Monon Bell game. Distractions exist. In recent years, more media outlets have shown interest in the game, combining with other campus activities and conversations to make concentration difficult for players. Amid the chaos, Carlson rations his words, as if his supply were running out. Because of the stir the Monon Bell game preparations cause, he becomes even more focused and those words become even more measured.

He doesn't have time for silly phone calls, yet that doesn't stop his phone from ringing. And

Former Wabash president Thad Seymour was always ready to lead Wabash men in a cheer, as he did here in 1977. This was a fine season for Wabash, going 11-2 and finishing second in the Division III playoffs.

even though he knows what awaits him on the other end, he answers dutifully. "I get calls at 9 p.m. at night, and they usually start on the Monday of game week," Carlson says. "Sometimes, people call and say, "This is the first Wabash-DePauw game I am going to go to, so you better win." Others just want to chat. Often, though, they want to chat about some of the plays I can call or haven't called in the past. That's when I know it's Monon Bell week. The fans start thinking about it early. But I guess I prefer it that way than the other way. I wouldn't want them to stop calling, because then there wouldn't be any interest in the game."

That seems unlikely in this annual affair, where the buzz continues until kickoff. "People feel free to come up to me, as I'm walking onto the field or on the sidelines before the game, and say,

In a joint effort to promote the Wabash-DePauw rivalry in the early 1980s, this photo of the two school mascots was staged for promotional purposes. In Monon Bell games which lack suitable action for fans, the mascots and their costumes occasionally have fallen victim to attack by rivals. The Tiger's tail, for example, has been pilfered many times, while Wally Wabash's head has also been stolen.

"I'm here today, so win," Carlson says. "I'll be on the sidelines during warmups, talking to one of my quarterbacks, whatever. And I'll look and see someone who wants to tell me that they are here. Like, now we can start."

Carlson tolerates the overzealous fans because he knows they epitomize the excitement level the rivalry has created.

But he could do without another annual Bell tradition: The Alumni Roast held in downtown Indianapolis each year a few days before the game. Alums usually gather at a posh hotel for food, drinks and laughs. Mont came up with the idea of the banquet in 1962 to improve relations between the Wabash and DePauw coaching staffs. "Despite

Wabash faithful prepare for the 1974 Monon Bell kick-off.

63

all the rivalry," Mont says, "we really had a good relationship with the Wabash coaching staff."

In recent years, the gala has evolved in a test of quips, with each alumni group trying to outdo the other. Or perhaps out-insult the other. Whether it's Wabash alums calling DePauw coach Nick Mourouzis, Nick "Nervosis," or the DePauw alums chiding the Little Giants for their lack of female companionship, sarcasm rules. The mood stays light, the jokes stay merciless, and Carlson would prefer to stay at home. "By Thursday night, you've got your team basically ready to play," he explains. "Your game plan is set, your state of mind is getting geared toward the game, and you're a little bit tired and maybe a little grumpy. Now you've got to get in a car and drive 45 minutes to Indianapolis for a party where people make fun

of each other, including you. I can take that, it's part of coaching. Both coaches go through the abuse part. It's agony, I'd rather go to the dentist. It's the one thing I don't like doing as the head coach at Wabash. More than once, I've thought about calling in hoarse."

By the end of Monon Bell week, Carlson may not be the only one nursing a sore throat. Alums, students, professors and plain, old fans routinely strain their vocal cords in the spirit of the rivalry. And some, like Kilbane, strain more than that. "But," he concludes, speaking for former Little Giants and Tigers everywhere, "it's for a good cause: The Bell."

In 1982, the Monon Bell is hoisted in the air, while a young Wabash fan shows the Big Cookie bumper sticker which proclaims Wabash's victory: "10-0. We're #1."

CHAPTER FIVE

The Classics: 1960

It was a simple question for a simple poll, like the ones that ask you what Presidential candidate you endorse, how you feel about health care or what soft drink you prefer.

All the questioner wanted to know from DePauw football coach Tommy Mont was if he would attempt the brand-new, two-point conversion if it was needed to win a game rather than settle for a tie. The 1960 season marked the first year coaches had the option of placing the ball on the hash mark from two yards out after a touchdown rather than kicking the extra point.

"The papers called me and asked me," Mont recalls. "I said, "Sure, I would go for two.' "

Easier said than done.

Mont learned that answering reporters'

questions on the phone and answering ones in his own mind with time ticking away in the fourth quarter of a one-point Monon Bell game differ greatly. "Little did I know," Mont says, "that the first time that the two-point decision would actually arise would be against Wabash."

But it did. The battle between the Tigers and the Little Giants lacked the luster of some Monon Bell matchups, but not the intensity. Never the intensity. And, oddly, for some reason, the 1960 game between the Tigers and the Little Giants sticks in the memories of loyal alums from both schools as much, if not more, than some classic battles from the same or more recent era.

There was the "Golden Toe" victory in '55, the '63 shutout which marked a decade of domi-

"I'd suit up if the Coach would let me, hang it!"

BEAT WABASH

AND "BEAT" IT DOWN TO
PROGRESSIVE PRINTING COMPANY TO BUY
YOUR CHRISTMAS CARDS TODAY!

nance for DePauw; the Mud Bowl in '67; the "Win One for the Katman" game in '68; the *Sports Illustrated* game in '73; the ABC-TV game during Wabash's playoff run in '78; the DePauw upset in Pete Metzelaars' final game in '81; the Wabash blowout in '82; the comeback in '86; the 100th matchup in '93 and so, so many others.

But many former players, coaches and alums, some with joints as rickety as a rusty gate, recall the 1960 Monon Bell game as one that epitomizes the rivalry in terms of fun and ferocity. Neither team had much to gain or lose, but those who remember the game recall a tough, close contest

not decided until the final minutes.

"That may be the one I remember most," says longtime Wabash athletic director Max Servies, who has seen his share.

"It was my first year on the staff and we had them beat, but blew it." Wabash entered the fourth quarter nursing a 13-6 lead. That in itself was somewhat incredible considering the Little Giants came into the game overwhelming underdogs because they had won only once that fall, a 12-6 mid-season victory over Hanover. DePauw, on the other hand, prepared to put an exclamation point on an otherwise drab season. The Tigers owned a 2-5-1 mark before the game, not great but much better than their hapless opponents. Besides, the Tigers had retained possession of the prized Bell since 1955, quite a mountain of momentum in a series so level.

Now the Tigers were only minutes away from watching whimsical Wabash fans take a victorious march onto the field and take the Bell away from them. Then Wabash fumbled. "I can still see that son of a gun Bill Kinkade hit the Wabash fullback and make him fumble," says Ted Katula, the DePauw athletic director and current Tiger golf coach. "What a hit."

With possession of the ball, DePauw still sputtered. The Little Giant defense held its ground, forcing the Tigers into a fourth-down-and-short-yardage situation. DePauw lined up to punt, but had other things in mind.

Servies wasn't fooled. But it didn't matter. He was sitting in the pressbox wearing coaching togs, a long way from the Wabash defensive secondary which was under attack. "I was yelling as loud as I could, 'Watch the fake punt, watch the fake punt,'" Servies says with only a small laugh. "But whoever I was talking to on the phone put the phone down for some reason. He didn't hear

The victorious DePauw team of 1960.

me. Nobody heard me. So the DePauw guy fakes the punt and throws a pass for a first down. Their drive stayed alive. "If we had gotten word to the sideline to watch the fake, maybe we would have stopped them. And maybe it never would have come down to the two-point play."

Mont emptied his bag of tricks. But, then, when his team played Wabash, it seldom stayed full. "We did a few different things that day," Mont says. "The rivalry always brought that out."

The fake punt was not the last trick. DePauw moved the ball deep into Wabash territory. Time clicked off the clock. A little over four minutes remained. DePauw, an option team, baffled the tired Little Giant defense.

Only a few yards away from the goal line, senior quarterback John Rubush kept the ball on an option play. His lane to the end zone suddenly was blocked by a sea of Wabash red. He flung the ball to tailback 'Skinny" Dan Blunt, who dove into

the end zone to make the score 13-12. "I still don't know how he pitched the ball," Katula says.

With the score tied, Mont's mind raced. He remembered being asked THE QUESTION. Well, Tommy, would you use the two-point conversion to win the game or would you settle for the tie? He wondered. He waited. He wanted some help. Katula, an assistant in the pressbox at the time, knew the answer. Mont didn't ask him, despite reports later that Katula hid under the window when Mont looked up to the press box for help. Turns out Katula told that tall tale to a reporter later and the reporter took him literally. But even though Mont didn't ask, Katula knew only one option existed in a one-point game with Wabash the opponent. "We had the Bell, to begin with," Katula explains. "And the first rule for any coach in this series ought to be that any coach that goes for the tie in that situation ought to be fired. Fired. The fans would hang him."

Mont also knew what he should do. But he figured he would ask anyway. Ask the DePauw fans, that is. "I turned around and asked the crowd what to do," Mont says. "They said, 'Go for it!' So we made up our mind to go for it."

He didn't share details of that decision with the Wabash defense. The Little Giants prepared their kick-blockers to soar above the crowded line and get a hand on the extra point. They expected DePauw to kick for the tie because the Tigers lined up in the extra-point alignment. And, being a 1-7 team, the Wabash defense succumbed to trickery rather easily.

"Wabash fell for it," Katula recalls. "John (Rubush) took the ball, ran an option with the kicker as the pitch back, and dove for the end zone.

"All I saw was a puff and knew John was in. Then I saw a bunch of celebrating."

The fans, players and coaches reveled in the 14-13 win, the pinnacle of the 1960 season which saw DePauw lose more than it won. Still, this win, in this manner somehow cast an amnesiac spell over the Tiger clan.

The Tiger players only remembered beating Wabash, not losing to Butler, Valparaiso or Hope. The Tiger coaches only remembered having enough guts to realize the glory of winning another Monon Bell. And the Tiger fans only remembered being asked for their input with the game on the line, each rooter taking home a piece of the Bell and a part of the victory.

"That was the kind of game that highlighted this rivalry," Katula says. "But, wow . . . wow . . . you, know, there were a hell of a lot of them."

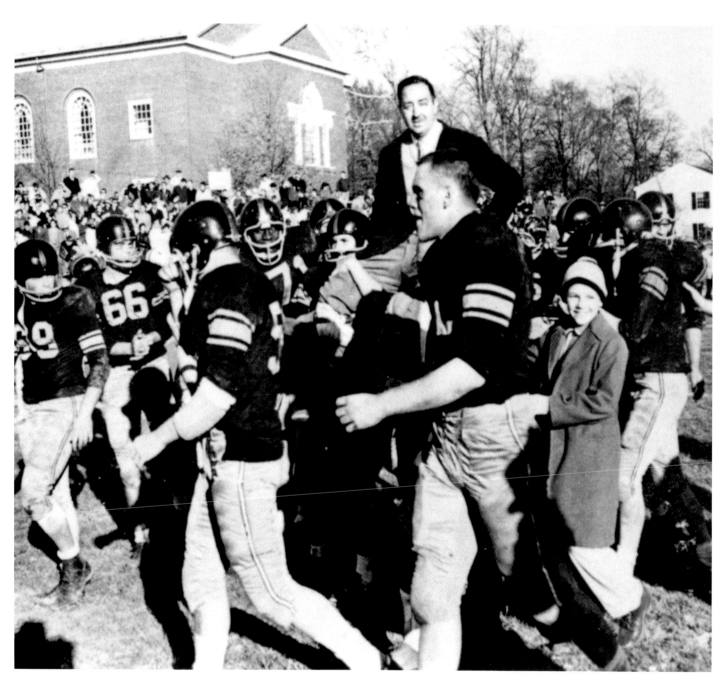

Coach Tom Mont gets the victory ride after DePauw's thrilling 1960 win.

The Bell arrives at the 1960 game in the traditional way...with a lot of security.

DePauw's Dave Clifford dives for the goal line in the 1960 Monon Bell game. The Tigers won for the fourth time in a row, this time by a score of 14-13.

The Tiger coaching staff, 1960: Left to right are Bill Graham, the student assistant, Head Coach Tom Mont, trainer Tiny Murphy, coach Bob Bataglia, coach Ted Katula, coach Edwin Snavely.

CHAPTER SIX

The Classics: 1985

Bumpers all over Montgomery County wore the same red-lettered warning. "The Big Cookie Says: A FUNNY THING HAPPENED TO THE DANNIES ON THEIR WAY TO THE PLAY-OFFS." Of course, these were the words and the wit of Rem Johnston, the "Big Cookie," the biggest Wabash College fan living or deceased. Johnston, a Wabash graduate and now a trustee, lives in Bluffton, Ind., and owns a printing company. Judging by the number of Little Giant posters, schedules and other memorabilia printed on his paper the past few decades, Johnston likes mixing business with pleasure. Most of his bumper stickers either congratulate or predict victory for Wabash, and occasionally they get down-

right pointed. One, for instance, stated simply: "The Big Cookie Says: "TO HELL WITH DEPAUW."

But in 1985, with the Tigers at 8-1 and Johnston's beloved Wabash a disappointing 6-2-1 entering the Monon Bell game, such malice may have been perceived as sour grapes, or worse, jealousy.

So the Big Cookie instead forecast failure for the tough-as-nails Tigers, who stood just one victory away from their first Division III playoff berth. It was only the second time the Tigers had climbed this close to the postseason.

But the one remaining opponent was, of course, Wabash, and while the Tigers cast their eyes

72

at blustery Blackstock Stadium on their first nine-win season since 1981, their hearts obviously were elsewhere. Probably keeping their minds company.

Crafty DePauw quarterback Tony deNicola detected trouble. And deNicola's antennae were seldom off the mark. This was a quarterback who started three seasons for the Tigers. This was a guy who wanted to play so badly against Wabash in the Monon Bell game his sophomore year in 1983 that he took the field with what doctors later diagnosed as three broken vertabrae. This was a pinpoint passer who had thrown five TDs in a game three times in 1985, including against Dayton only a week before the Monon Bell game. This was the leader of the Tigers, the man

Wabash running back Bill Kaiser set an NCAA Division III record by rushing 58 times in a 211-yard performance in the 1985 Monon Bell game. He carried Wabash to a 28-8 win.

whose fingers not only gripped the laces, but monitored the pulse of the DePauw football team. Days before the last regular-season game of deNicola's senior year, that pulse sounded erratic, if not faint. "It was a very emotional week," deNicola recalls. "It was Senior Week and there were talks and parties and guys hanging the other quarterback (Wabash's) in effigy. It was BIG.

"I mean, to that point, about 50 percent of your time was devoted to that sport and now it was ending, even with the possibility of playoffs. It was the beginning and the end of a lot of things. "We were in the situation where we had just beaten Dayton at home (35-31) the week before. Dayton beat Wabash that year 51-6. Manhandled them. So this was a huge win. And we got banged up pretty good because it was so physical. So we went into the Wabash game emotionally drained and physically hurt when we should have gone in sky-high.

Tony deNicola led the Tigers to a huge win over Dayton the week prior to the 1985 Monon Bell game, but he came up short in this nationally-televised game.

"In the middle of the week, I could tell. I said to the other tri-captains that this was not good. We could tell people were taking Wabash for granted, however strange that seems. We were better on paper, much better. But our seniors knew that, against Wabash, that doesn't mean a dang thing. And we knew that something wasn't right."

They didn't discuss their worries with DePauw coach Nick Mourouzis. They figured Mourouzis, occasionally referred by fans and foes alike as "Nick Nervosis" for his nervous tendencies, had enough to consider. But Mourouzis, a natural worrier, picked up the same signals.

"We had just played Dayton in one of the most fantastic games I could ever remember," Mourouzis says. "I could sense going into the Wabash game that something was missing. I mean, hey, everybody (on the coaching staff) was talking about it."

Meanwhile, they were barely talking in Crawfordsville. Disappointing seasons can be a powerful muzzle. Although the Little Giants prepared for the Monon Bell matchup assured of their 10th straight winning season, fans and players labeled the season one of missed opportunity. Expectations had stacked high enough and wide enough to cover the 27 miles between Wabash and DePauw. But an unexpected 14-14 tie with Ohio Wesleyan to open the season and a heartbreaking 28-26 loss to Albion shattered any hopes the Little Giants held of a perfect season. Worse yet, the dreaded Dannies had been enjoying a wonderful season just down the road.

In a way, all the factors combined to humble the team that had expected bigger things.

Even so, nothing could have prepared the Little Giants for the humiliation they suffered in Dayton on Oct. 26 of 1985. The Flyers flattened

Wabash 51-6, the Little Giants' worst defeat since 1972. Players usually handle lopsided losses in one of two ways; they either relive every painstaking play or they laugh it off and think of something else, like the next game. Afterward, most of the Little Giant players laughed it off. But Wabash coach Greg Carlson wanted them to hurt. Carlson reamed his team at a spaghetti restaurant after the game because of the frivolous mood after the 45-point pounding. He challenged their pride. He appealed to their competitiveness. He screamed and yelled much more than he ever had.

"It was an embarrasment to lose that way to Dayton," Carlson says. "And we needed to wake up." So he sounded the alarm. A week later, a different Wabash team returned home and crushed Kentucky Wesleyan, 26-7. All that remained was

DePauw, a final chance to restore the Wabash pride, a final chance to fulfill broken promises, a final chance to stick it to their neighbor to the south.

A final chance to ring the Bell.

While DePauw searched for its edge at practice in the week before the game, Wabash sharpened its own. Enthusiasm leaked out of the practice field and spilled onto campus. A few Wabash students were arrested for spray-painting red "Ws" on DePauw property. The Big Cookie passed out his car decals. And Bill Kaiser rested. He would need it.

Nature helped Wabash, watering the Blackstock Stadium turf with a steady Friday night rain. Maybe the DePauw gods were sweating nervously. By Saturday afternoon kickoff, former DePauw coach Tommy Mont, in the Tempo Tele-

Dave Adich gets help from Tim Metzinger in bringing down a DePauw receiver. Wabash pass defense was great this day, with five QB sacks and three interceptions.

Mike Worthington and Tim Metzinger celebrate another big defensive play in Wabash's 28-8 win in Greencastle.

Though one of the finest quarterbacks in DePauw history, Tony deNicola on this day couldn't avoid the defense of Dave Adich and Mike Worthington.

vision broadcast booth, pronounced the weather fitting for Monon Bell football: damp and dreary.

Ball control and defense, Mont predicted, would be Wabash's keys to victory. It turned out that he and the Big Cookie would look like prophets before the day ended.

deNicola never found his rhythm; a penalty on the first play of the game proved to be an omen for the Tiger offense. A harassing pass rush applied by the Wabash trio of Carl Hampton, Mike Haugh and Mike Worthington denied deNicola the time to throw. On his back and on the run, he failed to be effective.

Meanwhile, Kaiser ate up minutes on the clock like they were Wheaties in a bowl. Incredibly, indefatigably, he carried the ball 58 times, which remains an NCAA Division III record. The junior from Jasper, Ind., gained 211 yards that day, and, at one point, received the handoff 24 straight times. Yes, 24. "Jesus, that kid was amazing,"

The only thing that slowed Wabash's grind-it-out 28-8 victory over DePauw in 1985 was this dog. Dogs, too, are a traditional part of the Monon Bell games.

deNicola marvels.

"I got accused of tailback abuse that day," Carlson kids. "But I asked him, 'Billy, are you tired?' And he never asked me to stop. He wanted the ball."

Not until Kaiser conked out on the bus ride back to Crawfordsville did his fatigue show. Amid a busload of raucous riders, Kaiser took a nap still wearing his shoulder pads while sitting in one of the rear seats.

One of the more celebratory Little Giants on that bus was kicker Joe Bevelhimer. All he did was kick a school-record five field goals in Wabash's convincing 28-8 victory over the Tigers.

But the most content passenger of all, besides the sleeping star,

may have been Carlson. For him, the ride back to Crawfordsville that afternoon was too short. He wanted the road to go on and on and on. He wanted to freeze that moment and bury it somewhere underground, perhaps next to the Bell. For him, it marked the completion of a journey, one that started in August far north in the land of lofty expectations, veered south to the land of missed opportunity, went farther south to the land of humiliation, but now had made its final stop on a gray November day at a place he had never been before as a coach.

It is a place he will always cherish.

"In my time at Wabash (since 1980), the '85 game was the most rewarding Monon Bell game because of the circumstances," he says. "It erased the embarrassment. It kept the Bell away from DePauw. And it kept our friends from having their best season ever.

"They had everything to play for. We had pride. And we won.

(Below) Downfield blocking was critical to Bill Kaiser's running success in this game. Here Ed Broecker and Mike Funk were ready to head downfield, even though Kaiser got tripped up behind them.

DePauw vs. Wabash:
Photographic Moments
From the '70s, '80s & '90s

The DePauw-Wabash rivalry. It used to look like this...

...now it looks like this. In the 1990 game played in Crawfordsville, four Wabash defenders hammer a DePauw receiver. But DePauw had the last laugh, winning a hard-hitting contest, 20-13.

The cover of the 1974 Wabash yearbook poked a great deal of fun at the festivities surrounding the football game; not everyone was amused.

Wabash quarterback Dave Harvey huddles with Coach Frank Navarro during the 1977 game.

Wabash's Randy Mellinger scores in the 1976 Monon Bell game. Doug Carl (#76) raises an arm in celebration.

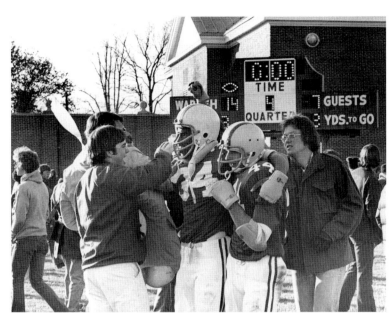

(Left) The 1976 game was won by Wabash 14-7, and they finished the year 7-3. Here, players Jimmy Parker (#34) and Greg Bussard (#44) are congratulated by the fans.

(Below) Wabash defender John Ruddy steps in front of the DePauw receiver and picks off a pass in the 1979 game. Wabash won this one, 16-13.

DePauw's Tracy Clifford, who passed for 1,666 on the season, barely gets one over the outstretched arms of Wabash's Bill Wheeler in the 1982 game in Crawfordsville. Both teams were strong this year, but Wabash won 31-6, and finished the year 10-0.

(Left) DePauw running back Rich Bonaccorsi eludes a Wabash tackler in the 1984 game. Bonaccorsi is DePauw's all-time leading scorer with 216 points, and is one of only a handful of players to start in the Monon Bell game all four years.

(Right) Victorious Tigers carry off the Bell after the 1987 game. The Tigers snapped a three-game losing streak with a 33-11 win, which started a string of four straight DePauw wins, the longest streak for DePauw since the early 1960s.

The Tigers charge onto the field for the 1980 Monon Bell game.

6,500 fans at Little Giant Stadium watched as Wabash's Rich Riddle gained ground in the 1984 Monon Bell game. Riddle ran for a touchdown and caught one as Wabash won, 41-26.

All friendships are off for the big game.

DePauw's Kevin Perkins was the MVP of the 1981 game, won by DePauw, 21-14.

Huddles of preparation for the 1986 Monon Bell battle.

Both Wabash (8-0-1) and DePauw (7-2-1) had great seasons in 1980, and the Monon Bell game didn't decide which team was better. Score it 22-22, in one of nine ties in Monon Bell history.

DePauw running back faces three Wabash tacklers in the 1986 game.

Wabash quarterback David Broecker looks for running room in the 1981 game. The Tigers won this one, 21-14.

The years may change, but the message for DePauw always stays the same. Here in 1980, it's carried by Coach Jerry Berndt.

DePauw kicker Dave Finzer, 1981. At the time of his graduation, Finzer held every DePauw punting and field goal record. He is also DePauw's third leading scorer with 81 career points.

(Above) Daryl "DJ" Johnson picks up yardage in the 1980 game. Johnson is the Wabash career rushing leader with 3,232 yards, which includes 1,000-yard seasons in 1980 and 1981.

(Left) Jim "Killer" Kilbane, one of the most prolific tacklers in Wabash history, stuffs another DePauw run, this one in the 1982 game. Kilbane wound up with 400 career tackles.

Tim Pliske kicks the winning field goal in the 1986 Monon Bell game.

Tight end Nick Crnkovich catches a pass during the 1982 Monon Bell game, won by Wabash.

(Above) This third-quarter touchdown made it 14-3 for DePauw in the 1980 game, but a determined Wabash comeback put the Little Giants ahead in the fourth quarter. With a minute to play, the Tigers scored a touchdown and a two-point conversion to salvage a 22-22 tie.

(Right) Dan Popravak picks up yardage in the 1980 game. After graduation, Popravak was instrumental in establishing the alumni game between the schools.

Wabash place-kicker Tim Pliske's field goal has just cleared the crossbar with 1:06 to play in the 1986 Monon Bell game.

The 1988 season saw the Little Giants ranked #1 in the nation for four weeks, before two losses, one of them to DePauw in this Monon Bell game, knocked them out of the national playoffs. All-American quarterback Brett Butler here waits for the snap as Tim Oliver, the first Wabash receiver to catch over 1,000 yards in passes, goes in motion. A fired-up DePauw upset Wabash 24-14.

DePauw's problems with their kicking game might have cost them the 1991 Monon Bell game. They had three extra points and a field goal blocked, and lost 23-18. Here, Eric Schoettle and Nick Ragsdale block one of the extra points.

(Above) David Broecker, First Team All-American and Academic All-American for Wabash in 1982.

(Right) Fred Kolisek punts to DePauw in the 1980 Monon Bell game, which ended in a 22-22 tie.

97

Spike Donahue confers with coaches on his headset during the 1982 game. DePauw went 8-2 that season.

DePauw and Wabash players clash on the first play from scrimmage in the 1982 Monon Bell game.

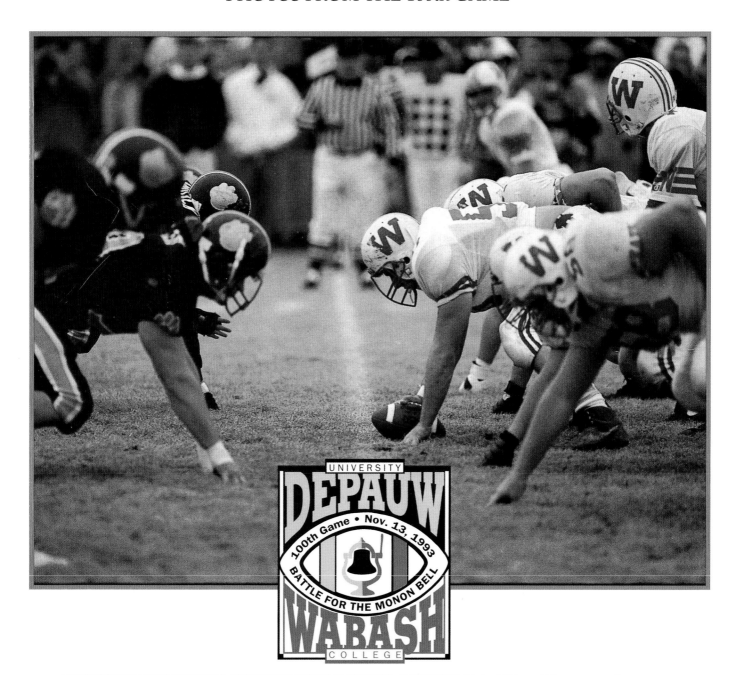

DePauw
vs.
Wabash College

November 13, 1993
(100th Game)

An annual event at Wabash Homecoming: Chapel Sing, at which pledge classes sing the words to "Old Wabash."

The Alumni Flag Game, an important part of Homecoming festivities.

Members of the Sphinx Club bring in the Bell before the start of the 100th game.

The DePauw band and faithful cheer as the DePauw Tigers reach the field.

Jason Shelton (#71), injured earlier in the year, prepares to lead the Little Giants onto the field.

The pre-game coin flip was attended by players, Booie Snyder '36 and Stuart Smith '33. Snyder caught the touchdown pass that beat DePauw in 1934, and Smith played in the first modern-era battle for the Monon Bell in 1932.

DePauw players feel the tension before one of the biggest games of their football lives.

Assistant Coach Steve House and Defensive Coordinator Peter Germano give instructions during a timeout.

Fierce DePauw defense smothers a Wabash runner early in the game.

This photo tells you all you need to know about the intensity of the 100th Monon Bell Game. DePauw tacklers annihilate a Wabash rusher.

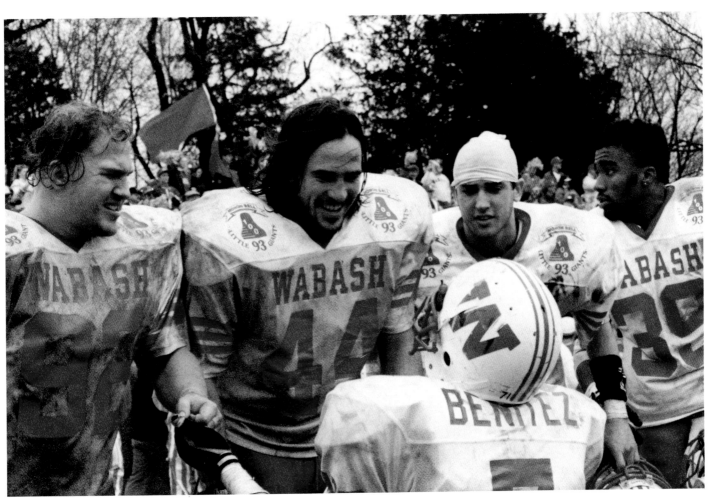

The Wabash defensive unit intercepted four passes, recovered two fumbles, broke up five passes, and had one quarter-back sack in a great season-ending effort.

Wabash ranked ninth nationally in Division III total offense, and these players can take a lot of the credit. This may be the best offensive line in school history. They are all smiles after Wabash's 40-26 win in 1993.

Wabash co-captain Andy Dorrel helps carry the 300-pound Bell off the field after the 100th game. Wabash's 40-26 win gives them the right to keep the Bell until the 1994 Classic is played.